THE YOUNG MARTIAL ARTS ENTHUSIAST

Tae kwon do – free sparring

Tae kwon do – an ax kick

Kung fu – the Crane

*Wu shu –
a graceful
movement*

*Judo – going
into groundwork*

THE YOUNG
MARTIAL
ARTS
ENTHUSIAST

DAVID
MITCHELL

Kendo – ready for practice

*Karate –
preparing for a
forearm block*

*Thai boxing –
fighting stance*

A DK PUBLISHING BOOK

Project editor Amanda Rayner **Art editor** Alexandra Brown

Photography Andy Crawford

Picture research Tom Worsley

Production Ruth Cobb and Josie Alabaster

Managing editor Anna Kruger
Managing art editor Peter Bailey

US editor Camela Decaire

This book is dedicated to Robin Lewis Peeler,
with thanks for her inspiration and encouragement.

First American edition, 1997
2 4 6 8 10 9 7 5 3 1
Published in the United States by
DK Publishing, Inc.
95 Madison Avenue, New York, New York 10016
Visit us on the World Wide Web at http://www.dk.com

ISBN: 0-7894-1508-9

Color reproduction by Colourscan, Singapore
Printed and bound by Lego, Italy

Contents

Important advice

Only a selection of the many martial arts techniques taught are featured in this book. You cannot teach yourself a martial art by following the sequences and moves shown on these pages. To learn the correct techniques you must attend a class run by a qualified instructor.

Introduction

THE FIRST MARTIAL ARTISTS developed their skills for use on the battlefield. Even today, most people learn a martial art for self-defense. You have to be very determined to succeed in the martial arts – it takes years of practice to learn the techniques. Students must prove their commitment through years of dedicated physical and mental training before they are even allowed to learn advanced techniques. However, there are many benefits, including improved fitness, increased confidence, and self-discipline. China, Japan, Korea, Thailand, Burma, Cambodia, Malaysia, Indonesia, and the Philippines all have traditional fighting arts.

Yin/yang symbol

The Chinese art

The Chinese martial arts are the oldest in the world, with some dating back more than 2,000 years. They are linked to religions such as Taoism, which uses the yin/yang symbol to show how strength should be balanced with compassion and gentleness.

A dojo in Japan

Japanese martial arts

The history of Japanese fighting systems stretches back more than 600 years. Kendo, or "the way of the sword," is one of the most ancient martial arts. Classes are held in a traditional training hall, called a *dojo*.

Buddhism

Self-discipline is essential for all martial arts practice and a serious state of mind is as important as physical fitness. Religions such as Buddhism have always played a major part in increasing self-awareness and control.

Golden statue of Buddha

The Shaolin Temple

The Shaolin Temple in Hunan Province, China, is the most famous place in the martial arts world. It is believed to be about 1,600 years old. The Shaolin monks were renowned for their fighting abilities and traveled throughout the Far East, introducing their art to many countries.

The Shaolin Temple, China

6

The Korean arts

In 1909 Japanese troops invaded nearby Korea and introduced the martial arts of karate, aikido, judo, and kendo. In the following years, the Korean people began to practice these martial arts and new forms gradually developed. A striking-based art called tang soo do developed from Japanese karate, and another Korean newcomer, hapkido, was inspired by Japanese aikido. In later years the Korean government tried to unite these systems under the name of *tae kwon do*, which means "the way of the foot and hand."

Tae kwon do

Samurai

The samurai were the soldiers of ancient Japan. To die in battle, in the service of one's lord, was considered to be the only fitting death for a samurai. They believed that a noble death would guarantee everlasting life in the next world.

Samurai warrior

Ninjutsu

Ninjutsu is a Japanese word meaning "the art of stealth." The ninjas were contract killers, hired to dispatch their victims usually with poison or by a knife in the back. The most successful ninjas were organized into secret families, or clans, and they remain mysterious figures to this day. Ninjas were so expert in the art of camouflage and concealment that many people believed they had the power to make themselves invisible.

A secret ninja hand sign

Kyudo

Kyudo means "the way of the bow." It is an ancient Japanese martial art that is now practiced as a form of mental discipline rather than sport. The unusual shape of the bow means that it can be used on horseback. Arrows are fired into a straw target and points are awarded for style in loading and releasing the arrow.

Kyudo demonstration

Eskrima

Eskrima is a traditional fighting art from the Philippines. Invading Spanish troops banned the use of weapons with blades, so a system of self-defense using single and double sticks was developed. Eskrima is now practiced throughout the world as a means of self-defense and as a combat sport.

Eskrima

Warming up

ALWAYS PREPARE for training with a carefully graduated series of exercises. Once you have warmed up properly by doing push-ups and running on the spot, you can begin stretching. When you have finished your martial arts training session, do not forget to cool down gradually with some slow stretching exercises.

What to wear

Each martial art has its own special training jacket. This type of jacket is worn for karate, tae kwon do, and tang soo do. Your martial arts school will probably be able to sell you a good quality jacket at a reasonable price.

If your hair is long, tie it back.

Do not wear any jewelry – it could get caught on clothing and cause an injury.

For most martial arts a loose jacket, or gi, is worn. Some schools have a special badge sewn onto the jacket to show membership.

Girls wear a plain white T-shirt under the jacket.

A colored belt is used to fasten the jacket at the waist. It is tied so that the ends are of equal lengths.

The pants are tied at the waist with a cord that is tucked inside.

Keep your fingernails short to avoid scratching your opponent.

It is important to keep your practice clothing clean and well-pressed. You must be neatly dressed for all martial arts classes.

Loose-fitting pants allow you to move freely.

For most martial arts the feet are bare to help you grip the floor. Make sure that your feet are clean and keep your toenails short.

1 Push-ups

Push-ups are good for developing muscle power in the arms, shoulders, and chest.

If you find ordinary push-ups difficult, drop your knees onto the floor to make them easier.

Bend your elbows until your chin touches the floor. Then push up fully until your elbows are straight. Try to do about 20 push-ups.

4 Toe touches

First touch your left foot with your right hand. Then switch sides and touch your right foot with your left hand. Do not straighten up between stretches.

If you cannot reach your toes, aim for your ankle instead.

Position your feet more than shoulder-width apart and reach for your left foot with the fingertips of your right hand. Repeat this stretch on the other side. Try to do at least 10 toe touches on each side.

7 The rack

This stretch is particularly useful for the striking-based martial arts.

Advanced stretches
Make sure that you have warmed up thoroughly before you try any advanced stretches.

Drop onto your hands and knees and separate your knees as widely as you can. Walk forward and backward on your hands several times. Try to hold the knees-spread position for at least a minute.

2 Twisting sit-ups

Twisting sit-ups are good for working the stomach muscles.

Lift your left knee and bring your body up and forward to meet it. Twist your trunk to the left and touch your left knee with your right elbow. Now repeat this on the other side. Try to do about 20 sit-ups.

3 V-sits

Put your hands on either side of your head.

V-sits work the stomach muscles very hard.

Raise both knees to your chest and bring your body forward to meet them. Try to do 20 V-sits, but do not worry if you can only manage a few at first.

5 Assisted stretch

Your partner stands on your left pant leg to stop your foot from lifting.

Keep your knee straight as your leg is stretched.

Lie on your back and lift your right foot. Your partner takes your right ankle and gently pushes it. Tell her when your leg has gone far enough. Hold the stretch for at least 10 seconds if you can, then change legs. Try to do 10 stretches on each leg.

6 Canoe stretches

Keep the backs of your knees pressed into the floor.

Sit facing your partner with the soles of your feet together. Press the backs of your knees into the floor and reach forward to take your partner's hands. Take turns pulling each other forward until your chin touches your knees. Try to do at least 10 pulls each.

8 Side split

Do not force the stretch and stop if it hurts. You probably won't be able to reach the full split position at first, but it will become easier with practice.

Slowly ease yourself into the split position.

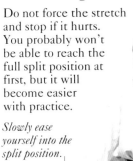

This type of split is sometimes called the box split.

If you regularly do this stretch, you will find it much easier to perform high kicks.

Sit on the floor and stretch out your legs on either side of you. Keep your knees straight and your body upright and place your hands in front of you for support. Try to hold the fully extended position for at least a minute.

9 Front split

The front split stretches the muscles at the backs of the legs.

Try to hold the stretch for at least a minute before you change legs.

Sit on the floor and stretch your left leg out in front of you. Now extend your right leg behind you. Keep your knees straight and your body upright and use your hands to help you balance.

Judo 1

JUDO IS A JAPANESE WORD meaning "compliant way." It is an Olympic sport and uses mainly grappling techniques. Competitors begin from standing positions and try to trip or throw their opponent. Points are awarded for clean throws, and you can follow your opponent down onto the mat to force a submission with a firm hold.

Back breakfall

The harder you slap, the easier you land.

Extend both your arms in front of you.

Bring your chin down into your chest.

1 Learn how to fall backward by taking up a squatting stance.

2 Roll back along the curve of your spine and slap down hard with both palms.

Low side breakfall

The first thing you need to learn is how to fall safely, so begin by squatting down.

Look directly ahead.

Hold your arms in front of you.

Spread your weight evenly between both feet.

Bring your right palm across your chest.

Kick your right leg forward.

Cushion your head against banging on the floor.

Fall to your right and slap down with your palm.

Counter to footsweep

You must learn to counter a footsweep by making good use of your opponent's energy. In this case your opponent has drawn you forward and tries to sweep your leading leg.

Keep your eyes on your attacker.

The attacker is firmly gripping your sleeve and lapel.

1 Your attacker tries a footsweep on you. She slaps the sole of her left foot against your right ankle.

She swings her left foot directly into your ankle.

Footsweep

This technique forces your opponent to take a step forward and sweeps her foot away as she is about to put her weight down onto it.

Grip her sleeve firmly.

She cannot stop herself from falling over.

Hold on to her wrist, or she will escape.

1 Hold your opponent's sleeve in your left hand and her jacket lapel in your right hand.

2 Draw your opponent forward and to her right. Stop her from moving her right foot by slapping into it with the sole of your left foot.

3 By drawing your opponent forward and preventing her from changing her foot position, you have forced her off-balance.

Do not lift your knee up too high or you will be vulnerable to attack.

You have stopped her footsweep.

She is about to fall over.

Her sweeping leg

With your foot raised, you cannot be tripped up.

2 Counter it by quickly lifting your right foot, so your opponent's left foot passes under it.

3 Now you can put her off-balance. Help her foot on its way by forcing her sweeping leg to one side.

11

Judo 2

J UDO THROWS use leverage rather than pure strength. Sometimes you can pull your opponent off-balance, other times you will drop below your opponent's center of gravity to topple him or her over you. Always keep a tight grip on your opponent so that he or she does not fall away from you.

Groundwork

Groundwork is the term used for techniques, such as locks and holds, that are performed on a judo mat.

Floating hip

For the floating hip you drop below your opponent's center of gravity and then lift him or her by straightening your knees. Once both feet are off the mat, you can put your opponent where you choose.

Leg reap

The leg reap unbalances your opponent and pushes him or her diagonally backward. Start by gripping your opponent's lapel and sleeve.

1 Pull your opponent toward you. As she resists, suddenly change direction and push her back.

2 Bring your right foot through and hook back with your heel and calf against your opponent's supporting leg.

Grip and push her right sleeve.

Opponent is in danger of overbalancing on her right foot.

Your heel hooks back.

Her supporting leg

Once you have started moving, do not stop because you are vulnerable.

Opponent

2 Turn so that your back faces your opponent and bend your knees. Then press your backside hard against him and straighten your knees.

3 Simply tip your opponent forward and over your hip so he lands flat on his back at your feet.

Keep hold of your opponent and control his landing.

Start with your knees bent, then straighten them to lift your opponent.

Both his feet are lifted off the floor.

Step through with your right foot.

1 Begin from a ready position by stepping through and across with your right foot.

Judo competitions
Throws in competition are rarely as clean as the ones you see in practice. This is because both competitors are highly skilled and have practiced the counter-movements many times.

Counter to leg reap

You can use this technique to stop your opponent as he or she tries to use a leg reap against you.

Opponent

Once in this position, you are ready to throw her instead.

3 Swing your opponent onto her back. Keep hold of her so that she cannot escape.

Grip your opponent firmly, ready for groundwork.

Your opponent is on her back. She will slap down to break her fall.

Your supporting leg

Step back quickly.

1 This time your opponent tries to use the leg reap against you.

2 Counter the throw by stepping back with your left foot and leaning forward.

Olympic judo
A top judo competition becomes a game of tactics. Both competitors are poised to look for and make instant use of a mistake by their opponent.

Counter to floating hip

You can counter the floating hip by sweeping your opponent's foot as he or she steps across to perform the throw. It is important to move quickly.

Be careful not to twist your opponent's wrist or you could damage the joint.

4 Keep hold of his wrist so that you can follow him down into groundwork.

Once he hits the floor, your opponent is in a vulnerable position.

Keep alert
Always watch your opponent closely and try to guess what his or her next move will be.

This requires perfect timing. Catch your opponent as soon as he steps in.

Slap the sole of your foot against his ankle.

Judo 3

NECK AND SHOULDER throws require a lot of leverage. Sometimes you will lift your opponent high into the air before dropping him or her at your feet. This technique scores a full point in competition. However, all neck and hip throws need a long lead-in, which makes you especially vulnerable to a counterattack.

Neck throw

The neck throw draws your opponent forward and off-balance because you jam his or her leg with your thigh.

Your hand is on his collar.

Opponent

Turn your back on your opponent.

His right leg is barred.

1 Put your right arm and hand on your opponent's collar and pull on his right arm as you quickly step across with your right foot.

2 With your back toward him, block your opponent's right leg so he cannot step forward.

Shoulder throw 1

This shoulder throw takes you under your opponent's center of gravity so you can lift him or her by simply straightening your knees. Then lean well forward, twist your body, and tip him or her over and onto his or her back. Be careful as you step in to make the throw because this is when you are most vulnerable to a counterattack.

1 Step across with your right foot and turn your back on your opponent. Release your right hand.

Trap his right arm by squeezing it hard with the powerful muscle in your upper arm.

Opponent

2 Drop under his center of gravity and push your right biceps muscle hard against the underside of his right arm. Grasp his sleeve with your left hand.

Bend forward until your back is almost horizontal as you throw him.

Bend your knees.

Step across with your right foot.

3 Bend sharply forward and lever him over your back.

Counter to neck throw

Now your opponent tries the throw on you. He slides his hand around your collar and steps in.

Lift his body into a horizontal position.

His feet are high off the floor.

Grip his belt tightly as he hits the floor so that he cannot escape.

With practice it will become easy to lift your opponent into the air.

Lean back slightly before you throw him.

3 Swing him over your right hip. Keep hold of his wrist as you dump him on the floor in front of you.

1 Hold your opponent's belt in your left hand and take control of him.

2 Bend your knees to get under his center of gravity and lift him off the floor.

3 Then dump him on the floor at your feet.

Counter to shoulder throw 1

Your opponent attempts a shoulder throw on you, stepping in and trying to jam his right arm under yours.

1 Bend your knees to lower your center of gravity and take a wide, stable stance.

Opponent

2 Straighten your knees and lift him high into the air.

Use your right hand to grip his left arm.

3 Tip him over and onto his back before you let him down.

Bend your knees.

Keep your feet wide apart.

Judo 4

GROUNDWORK is all about gaining the advantage when one or both of you have fallen or been thrown onto the mat. You may try to hold your attacker down by immobilizing him or her in some way, or you can apply leverage against a joint to force a submission. Ease the pressure as soon as he or she submits to avoid injuring your opponent.

Use your left hand to pull his right sleeve.

Bend your knees.

Step across with your right foot.

Shoulder throw 2

This shoulder throw makes good use of the standard lapel and sleeve grip. First you drop under your opponent's center of gravity as you turn in. Then, as you straighten your legs, you lift your opponent high into the air.

1 Keep a firm grip on your opponent as you step across and begin to wind in.

2 Bring your feet close together and bend your knees to drop under his center of gravity. Drag on his right sleeve and lift his lapel.

Cross arm lock

Use this technique immediately after a successful throw. Keep hold of your opponent's wrist at all times and then you can follow him or her down onto the mat to apply a submission hold.

1 You have thrown your opponent onto his back and wisely kept hold of his right wrist. Step in front of his head with your left foot and jam your right instep into his back.

The correct way to hold your opponent's wrist

Do not apply too much pressure or you will damage his elbow.

As you grip, be careful not to twist your opponent's wrist.

Position your feet on either side of your opponent's head.

2 Sit down and lean back, drawing his right arm over your thigh and over-extending his elbow joint. Keep your head up so that you can see what he is doing. Reduce the pressure on his elbow each time he taps the floor or your leg.

He will submit by tapping the floor when he starts to feel pain.

Push your hips back.

He is forced forward.

3 Drive your hips back and roll your opponent clear over your back.

In this counter throw you will both fall together.

Counter to shoulder throw 2

For this counter you use your hand to jam your opponent's hip and stop him or her from turning in fully. Then you bar both your opponent's legs and fall backward onto the mat together.

Keep a firm grip on his belt.

Bend your knees.

1 Counter the throw as before, preventing your opponent from stepping in.

Space your feet wide apart.

2 Then fall back with him and go directly into groundwork.

Scarf hold

For this hold-down you spread your legs as wide as possible and sink your body weight by bringing your head close to your opponent's. Lean heavily across your opponent's chest and hold tightly onto his or her jacket.

Spread your legs wide for maximum stability.

Position your right knee so that he will find it difficult to move.

The opponent may try to head-butt you.

1 This time your opponent has fallen at your side. Drop down onto your right knee, holding his shoulders with both hands.

2 Put your full weight on your opponent's chest and trap his neck in the crook of your right elbow. Grip his jacket firmly with both hands. Bring your hips to the floor and lower your head.

Grappling
Jujitsu is an ancient grappling-based martial art using throws, locks, and holds.

Jujitsu

JUJITSU, which means "compliant art," is all about using your opponent's strength to your advantage. It is a Japanese fighting system that includes punches, strikes, kicks, throws, holds, locks, and groundwork.

Escape from rear throat bar

Jujitsu works well at all ranges because it uses grappling as well as striking techniques. Here your opponent has come inside the range where a strike would be effective. Your only option now is to use grappling skills.

You will have to move quickly to avoid being strangled.

Opponent

1 Your opponent has seized you from behind, wrapping his forearm across your throat.

Escape from double lapel grab

The head-butt is a very dangerous technique and jujitsu is one of the few martial arts that teaches an effective defense.

Opponent has taken a firm grip on your jacket.

In this position he could try a head-butt or a kick.

Use both hands to force him away.

Now he cannot reach you with a head-butt.

His back is exposed to your attack.

You are about to bring your fist down.

1 Your opponent has taken hold of your lapels with both hands.

2 Step back with your right foot. Bring both hands up inside his forearms, turning your palms toward him.

3 Push his head down and bring your right fist up and back, ready for a hammer fist blow.

Self-defense
Jujitsu includes a great variety of techniques, making it very versatile as a method of self-defense. However, it has not lost contact with its traditional roots in feudal Japan. Jujitsu shares some of its origins with sumo wrestling and it is also the forerunner of modern judo.

Escape from side head lock

The side head lock is a common attack. Your opponent throws his arm around your neck and pulls your head in so that he can attack it with his fists.

Opponent

Use your right fist to punch his thigh.

1 Divert your attacker's attention by striking his thigh with a hammer fist.

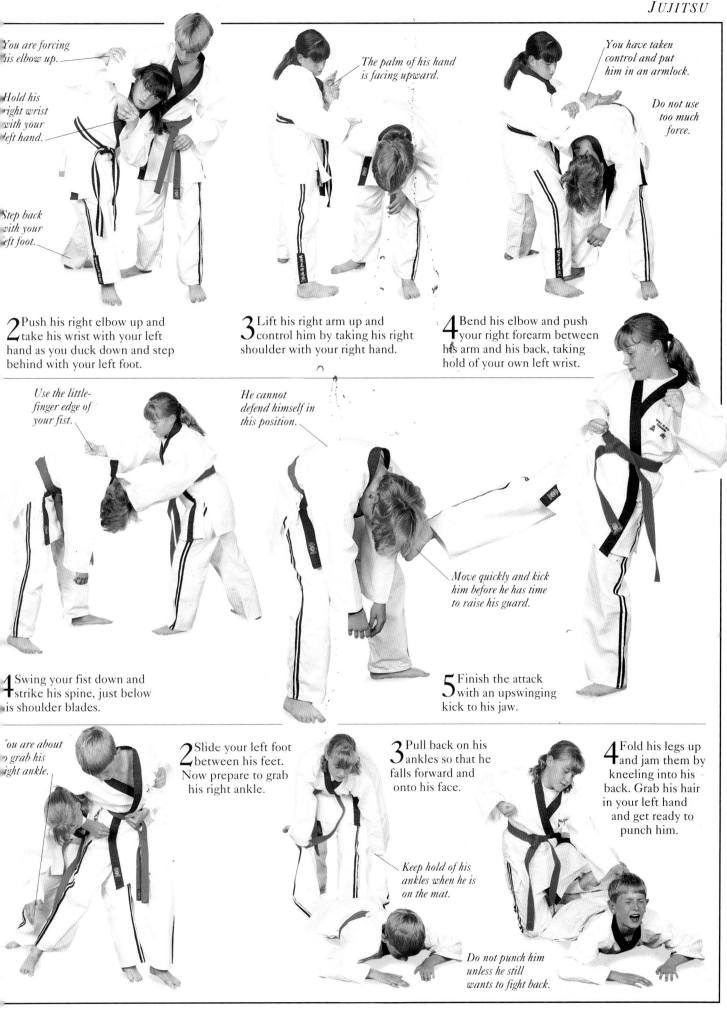

You are forcing his elbow up.

Hold his right wrist with your left hand.

Step back with your left foot.

2 Push his right elbow up and take his wrist with your left hand as you duck down and step behind with your left foot.

The palm of his hand is facing upward.

3 Lift his right arm up and control him by taking his right shoulder with your right hand.

You have taken control and put him in an armlock.

Do not use too much force.

4 Bend his elbow and push your right forearm between his arm and his back, taking hold of your own left wrist.

Use the little-finger edge of your fist.

4 Swing your fist down and strike his spine, just below his shoulder blades.

He cannot defend himself in this position.

Move quickly and kick him before he has time to raise his guard.

5 Finish the attack with an upswinging kick to his jaw.

You are about to grab his right ankle.

2 Slide your left foot between his feet. Now prepare to grab his right ankle.

3 Pull back on his ankles so that he falls forward and onto his face.

Keep hold of his ankles when he is on the mat.

4 Fold his legs up and jam them by kneeling into his back. Grab his hair in your left hand and get ready to punch him.

Do not punch him unless he still wants to fight back.

Aikido

AIKIDO MEANS "way of harmony." It is a grappling art that teaches you how to subdue your opponent without meeting force with force. By exerting pressure on the wrist, elbow, and shoulder joints, you can control your opponent and make him or her surrender. These are vulnerable areas and you must use care when applying the techniques to avoid injuring your opponent.

Self-defense
Aikido is a very beautiful martial art to watch and to practice because it includes many graceful movements. Aikido is also an effective fighting system that can quickly defeat even the most aggressive of attackers. It forms the basis of police self-defense and arrest systems in several countries.

Locking technique 1
The wrist is relatively weak and sensitive to pressure. Here your opponent has grabbed your lapel with his right hand.

Aim for his jaw to divert his attention.

Opponent

Ease the pressure on his wrist when he taps the floor, his leg, or your ankle.

A divided skirt, or hakama, is sometimes worn for aikido.

1 Take your opponent's wrist in an over-hand grasp and step back and around, so his elbow is straightened. Divert his attention by targeting his jaw.

2 Bring your left arm over his right elbow and hold his wrist. Use your right hand to exert pressure on his wrist joint.

Locking technique 2
The elbow is also sensitive to pressure.

Opponent

Keep your guard up as you prepare to defend.

You have forced him backward.

He is pulled forward and off-balance.

1 Face your opponent with your guard up.

2 He steps forward with his right foot and tries to grab you. Use his forward movement to add power to your attack.

3 Hold his right wrist in your right hand and step back with your left foot.

Deflecting a kick

In aikido you do not meet force with force. Rather than blocking your opponent's quickly rising leg, you simply lift it even higher to knock him off-balance.

Keep your guard raised to protect your body.

Opponent is about to try a front kick.

You are forcing his leg up to send him toppling backward.

He will use a breakfall to land safely on the mat.

He is off-balance.

1 Take up your guard as your opponent lifts his right knee, ready for a front kick.

2 Slide your right foot around as he kicks, so you are both facing the same direction. Now scoop up his kick with your left hand to topple him.

He has been forced onto one knee.

He cannot escape from your grip in this position.

3 Keep pressing down on his elbow and against his wrist, and squat down. This forces him onto the ground.

4 Keep a firm grip on his wrist and push his elbow down so he is forced to fall forward onto the ground. Ease the pressure when he submits.

The flowing art

Aikido is a moving, flowing art, which means that you never stand still for your opponent to hit you. Move as soon as your opponent does and once you make your response, do not allow your opponent to regain the initiative.

Use your left hand to steady his elbow and stop him from pulling away.

Your right thumb digs into the palm of his hand.

Grip his right wrist firmly with your right hand.

By pressing on his right elbow, you force him onto his knees.

Use both your arms to bend his elbow.

He has forced himself up again.

4 Keep him moving around as you step through with your right foot. Now press against his straightened right arm.

5 Maintain your grip on his wrist and arm and drop onto your right knee. Now bend his elbow.

6 Straighten up and bring him up on his toes by turning and lifting his right forearm.

Karate 1

KARATE IS A JAPANESE WORD meaning "empty hand." It began on the island of Okinawa and spread to the Japanese mainland in the early part of this century. There are four styles of karate, *shotokan*, *wado ryu*, *shito ryu*, and *goju ryu*, which differ from each other in small ways. Karate is a fighting system that relies mainly on high-energy punches, strikes, and kicks. The Korean martial arts of tae kwon do and tang soo do are both similar to karate, but use more kicks.

Courtesy – standing bow

You bow when you enter or leave the training room.

This is called the "attention stance."

Relax your shoulders.

Keep your eyes on your imaginary opponent.

This is called the "ready stance."

1 Put your heels together and your palms on your thighs.

2 Lean forward slowly and pause at the lowest point.

3 Return to an upright position, separate your feet, and clench your fists.

Making a fist

It is important that you make a correct fist so that you can hit a target hard without bruising your knuckles, hurting your fingers, or spraining your wrist. You can practice your punches against a pad held by your opponent.

1 Make a fist by closing your hand and locking it with your thumb.

Karate punches use only the index and middle knuckles.

Never enclose your thumb within your fingers – it could get broken.

2 Keep your knuckles in line with the bones of your forearm. This stops your wrist from bending painfully when you hit your target.

Punching on the spot

Begin from a ready stance by stepping to the left with your left foot, then to the right with your right foot. Bend your knees and sink into a horse-riding stance.

Look directly ahead.

Keep your body upright.

One fist faces up and the other faces down.

Sit low in a horse-riding stance.

1 Make two fists and push your right fist out and into the center. Twist it so that the palm faces downward. Next pull your left fist back to your side and twist it so that the palm faces upward.

Bend your knees.

Stand with your feet wide apart.

Courtesy – kneeling bow

This bow is performed at the beginning and the end of a karate class. Join the correct line for your grade and straighten your training tunic. Put your feet together and stand in an attention stance, with both hands flat against your thighs. When the class is settled, the senior student or instructor will call you to attention, ready for the kneeling bow.

Always keep your eyes on your imaginary opponent.

When you bow, bring your upper body forward with a smooth action. Pause at the lowest point before you straighten up again.

1 Drop onto your left knee, keeping your body upright.

2 Lower your right knee.

3 Sit back with your hands flat on your thighs.

4 Slide your hands forward and place them in front of you.

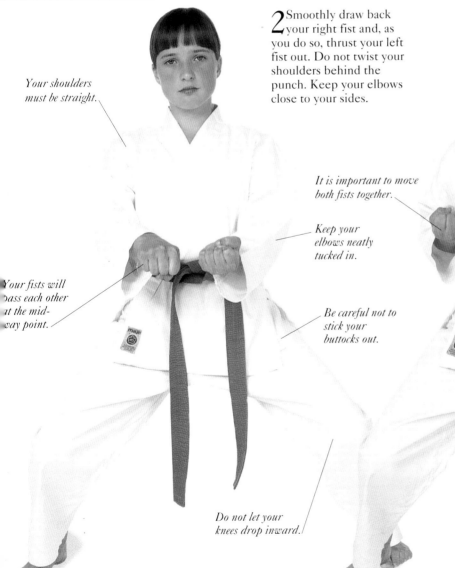

2 Smoothly draw back your right fist and, as you do so, thrust your left fist out. Do not twist your shoulders behind the punch. Keep your elbows close to your sides.

3 Continue drawing back your right fist and twist it palm-upward just as it reaches your hip. Keep thrusting the left fist out and into the center at exactly the same time. Twist the left (punching) fist so that the palm faces down.

Your shoulders must be straight.

It is important to move both fists together.

Keep your elbows neatly tucked in.

Your fists will pass each other at the mid-way point.

Be careful not to stick your buttocks out.

Do not let your knees drop inward.

As you push your left fist forward, twist it so that the palm faces down. Perform this action as you turn your right fist palm-upward.

Karate 2

KARATE TRAINING is split into seven parts: basic practice focuses on individual techniques; combinations are made up of two or more techniques linked to form a series; *kata* is a formal arrangement of combination techniques; in pre-arranged sparring both you and your opponent know the moves in advance; in semi-free sparring you know how your opponent will attack, but you choose the defense; in free sparring you both attack and defend as you wish; in competition points are awarded for good techniques against an opponent.

Reverse punch

Look directly in front of you.

Relax your shoulders.

Your front knee is bent and faces forward.

1 Begin from a left lunge punch position and punch with your right fist.

2 Keep your shoulders relaxed and your right arm still as you slide your right foot inward and forward.

3 Continue stepping forward and outward with your right foot and pull back your right fist as you come to a stop. At the same time, punch with your left fist.

Lunge punch

The lunge punch combines stepping forward with a punching action. The object is to time the punch so that it makes contact exactly as the advancing foot comes to a complete stop and you put your weight onto it. The lunge punch is performed from a deep, long posture known as a "forward stance."

Turning head block

Keep your fist in line with your forearm.

Remember to keep your fist in line with your arm so that your wrist will not bend when you punch.

Look over your left shoulder.

1 Begin from a left forward stance with your left fist extended.

2 Slide your right foot forward but keep your arms as they are. Both knees must remain bent, otherwise you will bob up and down.

3 As you finish your step forward, you pull back your left fist. Use this action to help thrust out your right fist.

4 Following on from the lunge punch, look over your left shoulder and slide your left foot across, raising your heel to make it easier.

Turning lower block

Bring your left fist back to your right ear.

With practice you will learn exactly how far to step across with your trailing leg.

Twist your hips to the left.

Blocking the kick
Do not try to block your opponent's rising shin square-on, or you might break your arm.

You can block the attack.

The attacker aims a kick toward your belt.

4 Following on from the reverse punch, lift your left heel off the mat and slide your foot across, making sure that you do not bob up as you do this. Bring your left fist back to your right ear.

5 Twist your hips strongly to the left, momentarily delaying your shoulder from following. This coils up the muscles in your spine and makes the following block much stronger.

6 Your block sweeps down and across, knocking your opponent's kick to the side.

Use both forearms to guard your face.

You must angle your forearm correctly to stop the blow.

The attacker cannot reach his target.

5 Twist around smoothly to face the other way, bringing both forearms across your face in a safety block.

6 Pull your right fist back to your hip, using this action to help power a rising forearm block with your left arm.

7 The angled forearm blocks an attacking technique.

Karate 3

BASIC KARATE TRAINING involves practicing punches, strikes, blocks, and kicks. There is a grading system of colored belts and beginners wear a red belt (although some clubs use white belts for novices). Next is the white belt, followed by yellow, orange, green, purple, and three grades of brown, then the black belt. There are also stages within the black belt called "dans," so a new black belt is a first dan and the most experienced in the world is a tenth dan.

Competition rules

Karate competition is very fast and is fought over a single bout of two or three minutes. Bouts are won by either competitor scoring a maximum of full points and/or half points totaling three points, or by scoring more points and/or half points than the opponent.

Knife block

This block uses the little-finger edge of the hand to deflect attacks. Keep your fingers fully extended and together, and press your thumb into the side of your hand. Start in a ready stance, then slide your left foot forward.

Forearm block 1
Middle inner forearm block

The forearm blocks use the full length of the lower arm to "wipe" an incoming technique to the side.

Extend your right fist forward.

Draw your right fist back to your ear.

This girl's green belt shows that she has reached the fifth stage in the grading system.

Bring your left forearm across your chest.

Begin with your left foot in front.

Slide your right foot forward to meet your left foot.

The right forearm is used for the block.

Draw your left fist back to your hip to power the block.

Step through with your right foot.

This block uses the part of the forearm that lies below the little-finger edge of the hand.

This is a left "cat stance."

Start with your left palm facing forward.

Bring your right palm to the left side of your face.

Your right hand is palm upward on your chest.

Bend your right knee.

Lift your left heel off the floor.

Your right foot is in front.

1 Place most of your weight on your right foot. Your left palm faces forward and your right hand is palm upward on your chest.

2 Step forward with your right foot and drop your left hand so that your fingers face forward.

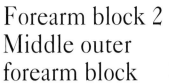

Forearm block 2
Middle outer forearm block

This is a difficult block that uses a windshield wiper-like action of the blocking forearm to knock an attack to the side. The thumb side of the forearm is used to make the deflection and the blocking hand rotates sharply just before the deflection is made.

Your palm faces down under your armpit.

Keep your hips straight.

Bend your knees.

Keep your left fist palm upward.

The attacker cannot reach you.

You have blocked your body.

1 Begin with your right foot forward and your left fist extended.

2 Slide your left foot forward and bring your left hand under your right armpit.

3 Move your left foot farther forward and draw back your right fist.

4 Use this action to power a block with your right forearm. Use the part of the forearm that is below the thumb.

This is a right-hand block.

Your opponent's body is slightly turned into the punch.

The left palm is upward and the hand is at chest height.

The punch is aimed at chest height.

The knife block is used to force the punch away from the body.

This is a right "cat stance" with the right foot in front.

Your opponent slides strongly forward with his right foot.

3 Continue the step forward into a right cat stance. As you finish the movement, draw back your left hand to your chest and turn it palm upward. Use this action to make the block with your right hand.

4 The block uses a cutting action with the little-finger edge of the hand. That is why it is called a "knife block."

Karate 4

KICKS ARE USED as middle- to long-range weapons. They are more powerful than punches, but kicks have to travel a long way to reach their target, so an alert person can avoid them. There are four basic kicks in karate. The front kick strikes with the ball of the foot, the roundhouse kick uses either the ball of the foot or the instep, and both the side and the back kick use the heel and little-toe edge of the foot.

Side kick

The side kick involves turning your hips away from the target and it can leave you open to your opponent's attack. Raise your kicking knee high to the side.

Aim your right heel toward your target.

Lift your big toe and turn down all the others.

1 Begin from a left fighting stance. Turn your left foot out and bring your right knee across your body.

2 Drive your heel out in a powerful, straight thrusting action. Pull the kick back and resume your stance.

Front kick

The front kick uses a thrusting action to drive the ball of the foot into the target. Raise the kicking knee higher than the height of the target and maintain a defensive guard throughout.

This is the fighting stance.

Your guarding fist protects your upper body.

This girl has achieved a black belt in the grading scheme.

Bend your knees.

Keep your fist up to guard your face.

Aim the kick toward your target.

It is important to pull your toes back in the kick. This prevents possible injury.

The ball of your foot lies just behind the toes. It is good for kicking because it is a hard area. (You could hurt yourself if you tried to kick with your toes.)

Bend your left knee.

1 Begin in a ready stance and slide your left foot forward a short distance. Bend both knees equally and carry your fist in a realistic guard.

2 Change your guard so that your right leg leads and bring your right knee forward and up. Pull your toes back.

3 Keep your supporting leg bent as you thrust out the ball of your right foot. Pull the kick back and set your foot down gently.

Roundhouse kick

The roundhouse kick is one of the most popular techniques in karate. You can strike with either the instep (toes fully extended) or the ball of the foot. This kick is different from the other three basic kicks because it curls around horizontally into the side of the target.

1 Begin from a left fighting stance.

Remember to bend your knees slightly.

Point your toes as you get ready to kick.

Aim the kick toward your imaginary opponent's head.

Keep your elbows close to your sides.

Allow your supporting foot to swivel freely.

2 Change your guard and bring your right knee up and across your body.

3 Twist on your supporting leg and kick horizontally across the front of your body. Pull the kick back and set your foot down carefully.

Back kick

The back kick involves a powerful twisting action to spin the body around. However, turning your back on your opponent can be dangerous, so only use a back kick as a surprise move, or after another attacking technique.

Keep your guard up to protect your face.

Aim your heel toward your target.

Keep your eyes on your opponent.

The distance you slide your leading foot across before you kick will determine whether or not it is on target. Knowing the correct distance to step comes only with lots of practice.

Twist at the waist.

When you finish a kick, always put your foot down in a controlled way.

1 Begin from a left fighting stance by sliding your left foot across.

2 Twist to look over your right shoulder.

3 Pick up your right foot and thrust it straight back, heel first, into the target. Pull the kick back and continue turning on your left foot.

Karate 5

Opponent in a left stance

Carry an effective guard at all times.

Do not warn your opponent of your intentions.

D O NOT TRY free sparring until you can perform the basic techniques with confidence. Not pulling your toes back for a front kick can be extremely painful. Always work with your opponent – that way, both of you will learn together. Most importantly of all, always control your techniques so that your opponent is not injured.

Free sparring – combination 1

This combination uses two different hand techniques.

1 Take up a right fighting stance while your opponent is in a left stance.

Free sparring – combination 2

This combination uses hand and foot techniques in a fast sequence. The punch to the face hides the slide-up of the attacker's leg.

Watch your opponent carefully.

She blocks your punch with her palm.

The punch into her face hides the slide-up of your left leg.

Opponent's left foot in front

You lead with your right foot.

1 Begin from opposite fighting stances.

2 Throw a fast face punch, using this to hide the slide-up of your trailing leg. Your opponent slaps your punch off course with a palm block.

Your opening punch distracts his attention.

Slide forward with your right foot.

2 Slide forward with your right foot and thrust a reverse punch with your left hand at your opponent's stomach. Then bring your right arm back to your ear.

The back fist is unexpected.

3 Use the pull back of the spent punch to power a back fist strike with your right hand into your opponent's head. Allow your trailing foot to slide up.

She gets ready to counterattack.

Smack hard into your opponent's lower leg with your shin.

3 Jar your opponent's leading foot with your right shin, as though trying to unbalance her.

Keep your shoulders relaxed as you kick.

4 Draw back your right foot, point your knee at the target, and snap out a front foot roundhouse kick.

Kendo

KENDO means "the way of the sword." It is a form of Japanese swordfighting that began more than 650 years ago. In those days, armored warriors fought with swords. However with the introduction of the gun, the sword fell out of favor.

The top part of the body protector is the mune.

A jacket, the kendo-gi, is worn.

The do is made of hard plastic or bamboo and guards the chest and middle.

The scarf, or tenegui, is used to cover the head.

The tsu is the hi guard

Armor

When you have put on your armor and taken up your practice sword, you are ready to begin.

Kote, or padded gloves

The shinai is a bamboo practice sword. Place the hilt guard in line with your knee.

Preparing for kendo

To practice kendo, you will need a special head guard, a chest and middle protector, padded gloves, and a bamboo practice sword. Each time you train, you must place your equipment close to you and take up a seated position to put it on.

The metal bars of the mask protect your face and let you see out.

The scarf cushions against blows, protects your hair, and soaks up sweat.

The men, or head guard

The shoulder protectors are part of the head guard.

Throat protector

Scoring cuts

In competition, points are awarded for hitting scoring areas with the correct technique.

The right hand controls the direction of the sword.

The left hand is used to power the sword.

The correct way to hold the practice sword

1 Parry (catch) your opponent's practice sword with yours to stop his forward movement.

Divided skirts, or hakama, are worn. They allow you to move freely.

The feet are bare.

Targets

You can follow step 1 by cutting down on your opponent's head guard (a), body armor (b), or glove (c).

Opponent

Take a big step forward with your right foot.

Try not to move your hands on the handle.

The men *is the target for this cut.*

Always grip with both hands as you strike.

Keep your elbows up.

Step forward as you hit the target.

1 Bring your sword back over your head and spring forward with a yell.

2(a) Strike a solid blow on the top of your opponent's head. Do not worry – the head protector will stop him from being hurt.

The padded gloves reach almost to the elbows to protect the forearms.

The do *is the target for this cut.*

You can score on either side.

Cutting down
Try to keep your left hand in line with the center of your body as you cut down.

The kote *is the target for this cut.*

You will not need to take a big step forward for this cut.

2(b) Another way to score points uses a strike into the side of your opponent's body armor.

2(c) You can also score by cutting down on your opponent's right wrist.

---

2 Step diagonally forward to the right and hit your opponent's body armor with a loud shout.

From this position you will turn to face your opponent, ready to strike.

Grip the handle with your right hand nearest the hilt guard.

His right side is hit by the practice sword.

3 Follow on through by stepping past, then turn around to face your opponent once more.

The hip protectors, or tare, *have slits at the waist to let you bend easily.*

Step forward with your right foot.

Your leg movements are hidden by the hakama, *so your opponent cannot guess your next move.*

Kobudo and Iaido

The tonfa were originally rice grinder handles, but they make very effective weapons. They can be butted into an opponent, or swung around and used as a baton.

KOBUDO MEANS "old martial way." It makes use of converted agricultural tools from the island of Okinawa near Japan. They include the threshing fork, rice flail, and grinding wheel handles. Iaido is the art of drawing and using a Japanese sword. Iaido is practiced without an opponent. In medieval times, swordfights were often won by the first person to draw his sword.

Iaido

The sword must be the correct length for the person using it. First the sword is drawn smooth then a cut is made. Next the blade is shaken – originally this would have removed the enemy's blood. Finally, the blade is returned to the scabbard with a flourish.

The scabbard is the hard case in which the sword is stored.

The hakama is the traditional divided skirt worn for practicing iaido.

1 Take up a ready stance with your left hand at the top of the scabbard and your right hand resting on the sword handle, close to the finger guard.

The sais

The *sais* (not shown) originally came from a type of threshing fork used in farming. They are always used in pairs and can be used to stab or to club the opponent. They are also handy for reinforcing your elbow during a block.

The nunchaku

The rice flail, or *nunchaku*, is an extremely effective weapon. This sequence shows the rice flail in use.

Quickly wrap the rice flail around his ankle.

The attacker tries a front kick to your midsection.

Keep your head well away from your attacker.

He is trying to punch you.

1 Here the rice flail is being used to stop your attacker's front kick.

2 Quickly wrap the flexible linkage around his leg.

Imagining your opponent
To make iaido meaningful, you must concentrate and picture your opponent in your mind's eye. Only then can you develop the correct mental attitude.

Part of the sword blade is now exposed.

The iaido sword has a blunted blade.

Make a downward cut with the sword.

Grasp the handle with both hands.

Take your time and be very careful as you return the sword to the scabbard.

Hold the top of the scabbard steady with your left hand.

2 Slide your right foot smoothly forward and begin drawing the sword.

3 Grasp the handle with both hands as the blade comes free. Now bring the sword around and into a downward cut.

4 When you have made the cut, hold the top of the scabbard in your left hand and slide the blade smoothly back and into it.

You have twisted him around.

He is in a vulnerable position with his back to you.

Aim a kick toward his midsection.

He has fallen forward.

3 Tighten the linkage around his shin and twist him around. Be careful not to damage his ankle.

4 Lift the batons to up-end him and finish the sequence with a well-placed kick.

Tae Kwon Do 1 Side kick

TAE KWON DO MEANS "the way of the foot and fist." It is a modern Korean fighting system similar to Japanese karate. However, tae kwon do is an Olympic sport and it is justly famous for the quality and number of its kicks. Many people believe that tae kwon do kicks are the best in the martial arts world.

As you become faster and faster, the step will blur int a sideways hop.

The belt has flown up with the force of the kick.

Leading foot

1 Begin from a fighting stance with your arms in a relaxed guard.

2 Step quickly behind your leading foot, so your hips swivel away from the direction in which you are moving.

3 Thrust out your hee and the little-toe edge of your foot in a powerful side kick.

Ax kick

This is an ax kick, in which the foot is swung high above your opponent's head before being dropped heel first onto his head or collarbone.

Your opponent keeps his guard up to protect his collarbone.

Use the arm opposite your kicking leg to help you balance.

Jumping front kick

Jumping kicks are made when both feet are clear of the floor, so first you have to be able to jump up high. Always tuck up your non-kicking foot, kick as you are rising into the air, and keep control of your guard. Land in a defensive posture with an effective guard.

Use your fists to guard your upper body.

1 Try your first jumping kick from a high stance with both knees bent.

Bend your knees.

Skip front kick

A skip change means switching your feet over just before you kick. The skip makes the kick more powerful and the change of stance confuses your opponent.

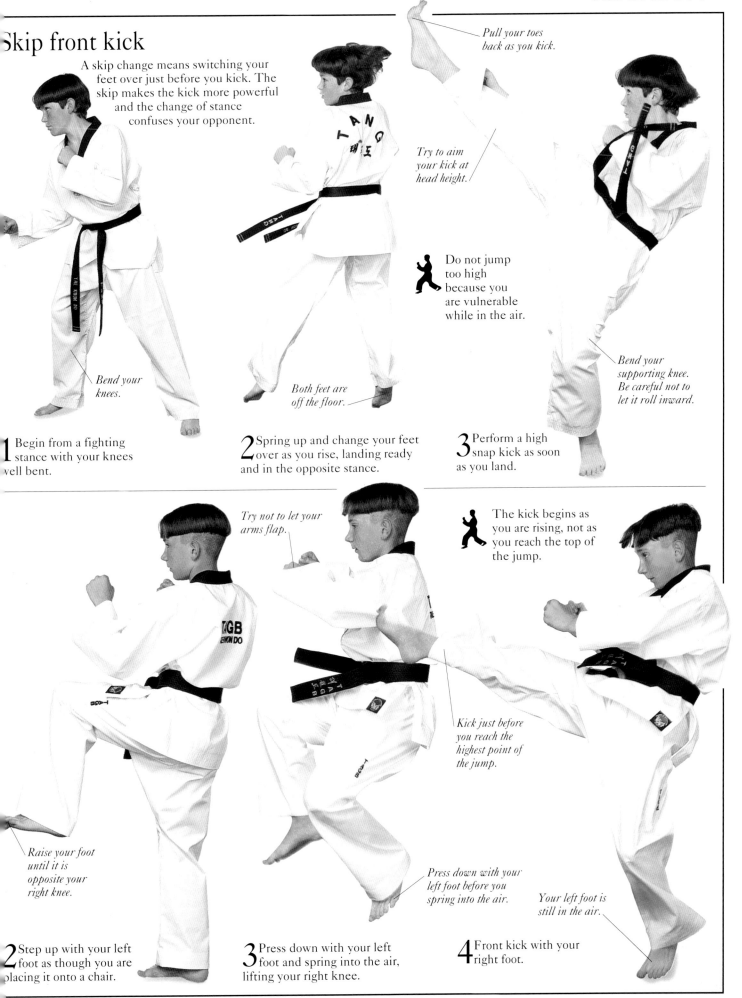

Pull your toes back as you kick.

Try to aim your kick at head height.

Do not jump too high because you are vulnerable while in the air.

Both feet are off the floor.

Bend your supporting knee. Be careful not to let it roll inward.

Bend your knees.

1 Begin from a fighting stance with your knees well bent.

2 Spring up and change your feet over as you rise, landing ready and in the opposite stance.

3 Perform a high snap kick as soon as you land.

Try not to let your arms flap.

The kick begins as you are rising, not as you reach the top of the jump.

Kick just before you reach the highest point of the jump.

Raise your foot until it is opposite your right knee.

Press down with your left foot before you spring into the air.

Your left foot is still in the air.

2 Step up with your left foot as though you are placing it onto a chair.

3 Press down with your left foot and spring into the air, lifting your right knee.

4 Front kick with your right foot.

Tae Kwon Do 2

A MAJOR PROBLEM when performing a jumping kick is that you can lose your sense of direction and miss your target completely. This is why you must always keep your eyes focused on where the kick is going. In kicks such as the jumping/spinning back kick, this is not always easy. Twist your head quickly to look over your shoulder so you lose sight of the target for the shortest possible time. Also, the greater the number of movements you have to produce in the air, the higher you must jump to fit them all in before you land.

Jumping/spinning back kick

A jumping or spinning back kick is one of the most difficult of all the airborne kicks.

Thust your right heel toward your target.

Look over your shoulder to check where your opponent is.

Begin with a jump high into the air, with your left foot leading. Then twist clockwise so your back faces your opponent.

Then pull the kick back and continue turning. You will land with your knees bent, facing your opponent.

Wedging block

Blocks use hands, arms, and knees to force incoming techniques away from their targets. To minimize the risk of injury, swing your block into the side of the attack and never directly into its path.

The attacker is about to punch you with both fists at the same time.

Your fists are at waist height.

Push her arms apart just above her wrists.

Space your feet wide apart so that you remain stable.

1 In the wedging block you use your forearms against your opponent's double punch. Get ready to block by drawing both fists palm-upward to your hips.

2 Thrust both fists forward, turning them at the same time, so the palms face your opponent and her arms are knocked outward.

imagine that you re putting your ot up on a chair.

1 Step up with your left foot and pring off the floor vith your right foot.

2 Turn while you are in the air and bring your kicking knee forward. This bent-knee position before a kick is called the "chamber position."

Your right leg is ready to kick.

Tuck your supporting leg under you as you jump.

3 Now kick out with your right shin and instep to perform the full kick. Keep your eyes on your target and land in a prepared position.

Flying roundhouse kick

The flying roundhouse kick is a difficult technique to perform because first you jump and twist one way, and then you twist the other way as you perform the kick. Remember to tuck up your supporting leg and keep control of your arms.

This kick is similar to the roundhouse kick in karate (see page 29) but has an added jump.

She may try a head-butt.

Be careful not to bring your head too close to hers.

Shout as loudly as you can while you attack.

The solar plexus, at the pit of the stomach, is vulnerable to attack because it has many sensitive nerves.

She cannot defend herself in this position.

3 Now take your opponent's shoulders in a firm grip.

4 Drive your left knee into your opponent's middle. Let out a shout, called a "kihap," as you do this to concentrate force and effort into the strike.

Tae Kwon Do 3

TAE KWON DO USES different drills to help you practice safety and improve distance, timing, and accuracy. In prearranged sparring, you and your opponent decide who will attack, which technique will be used, and what the defense will be. Your opponent makes three or five consecutive attacks with the same technique, and on the final defense, you follow with an agreed counterattack.

Reverse knife hand strike

Here your opponent has stepped strongly toward you with her left foot.

1 Your attacker tries to punch you with her right fist. Draw your body back into an "L" stance and deflect the punch.

Opponent

Deflect the punch with the little-finger side of your forearm.

Make an "L" shape with your feet.

Hooking kick from grasp

Most people regard kicks as long-range weapons. Kicks can also be used from short distances – but only after your opponent's chance to counterattack has been neutralized. Drawing your opponent off-balance is a good way to neutralize a counterattack. Otherwise you can step to a closed side before kicking. Be very careful about kicking someone when you are in punching range because a punch will always reach its target first.

1 Your attacker steps forward with her right foot and tries to punch you with her right fist. Draw your body back into an "L" stance and curl your hand over her wrist, closing your fingers and holding on tightly.

Opponent

Hold her wrist firmly so that she cannot pull away from you.

Pull back into an "L" stance.

Vertical back fist from grab

This sequence is taken from a form of training that is normally practiced without an opponent.

1 Your attacker has taken hold of your right wrist.

She is grasping the top of your wrist with her left hand.

2 Extend your fingers and use the strength of your body to pull your wrist free.

You have pulled away.

Bend forward from the waist.

Your left fist is to the outside of your right hand.

3 Draw back your left fist, using this action to help power a knife hand strike to the side of your opponent's head.

2 Cross your arms in front of your upper body and close your left hand into a fist. Hold your right hand open, with your fingers extended.

Aim for the side of her head.

2 Lift your right foot and flex your ankle, ready to kick.

Lift your right foot.

Your hips are already turned away.

3 Lean away and hook your heel high and around into the back of your opponent's head.

Hold your left fist up to guard your body.

Keep your eyes on your opponent.

Your palms are facing away from you.

3 Spin counterclockwise and draw your feet together. Cross your forearms in front of you with your right arm nearest your body.

Your feet are together.

Shout loudly as you strike.

4 Slide out with your left foot and strike your opponent with a left back fist to the side of her head.

Tae Kwon Do 4

THERE ARE TWO different types of tae kwon do, each with its own rules for competition. Olympic tae kwon do allows full power kicks to the body and head, and full power punches to the body. ITF tae kwon do scores with much lighter impacts.

1 Face your opponent in fighting stance.

Keep your guard up.

A head guard cushions blows to the head.

Keep your head up so that you can see what your opponent is doing.

It helps if you lean back when you kick high toward your opponent's head.

Reverse turning kick

The reverse turning kick uses a 180 degree turn of the body.

ITF tae kwon do

International Taekwondo Federation competition involves fairly low impacts wearing head, fist, and foot protection. It is practiced by groups that follow the teachings of General Choy, an early pioneer of the martial art. It is a lot of fun, although it can be fairly tiring. ITF tae kwon do is the safer of the two forms, especially for young people.

Hand guards protect the fists. A piece of elastic keeps the hand guard securely in place.

Safety points

• Do not attempt free sparring until you are confident in the basic techniques of tae kwon do.

• You must use control to limit the impact of techniques against an opponent.

• Practice kicks, strikes, and blocks to develop accuracy and to improve timing and your ability to judge distances.

Foot protectors cover the tops of the feet (the part used for most kicks).

Scoring points

The object is to score points with skillful techniques delivered to scoring areas of your opponent's body.

Keep your eyes on your opponent at all times.

This twisting action sets up a rubber band-like tension in the muscles of your spine and trunk.

Remember to keep your guard up.

Draw your toes back.

4 Now hook strongly back with your heel in a spinning reverse roundhouse kick.

2 Twist your body strongly clockwise and allow your feet to move naturally. Look over your right shoulder.

3 Begin turning your hips and lift your right foot into a chamber position, ready to kick.

She bends her knees to avoid the kick to her head.

Olympic/WTF tae kwon do

Olympic or World Taekwondo Federation tae kwon do uses full contact blows and kicks to the body and head. Punches into the face are not allowed. Matches can last up to three rounds, so they demand a very high level of fitness.

Watch your opponent as you perform any jumping kick.

A head guard protects against very high kicks.

Keep your guard up.

This is a flying side kick to the chest.

A body protector, or hogo, is worn for practice with an opponent.

Bend your supporting knee.

The kicking leg has reached full extension.

Kicks to the body are one of the most important attacking techniques.

Scoring points

The object is to score points with a solid hit that knocks your opponent down. You have to be brave to take part in this sort of competition.

The shin/instep guards protect your feet as you deliver powerful kicks.

All competitors wear a groin guard.

Olympic sport

Tae kwon do will be introduced as an Olympic sport in the year 2000 at the Sydney games. Judo is the only other martial art with Olympic status.

Shin/instep protectors are specially padded.

43

Hapkido and Tang Soo Do

H APKIDO AND TANG SOO DO are both Korean fighting systems. Hapkido means "way of harmony," and it includes striking and grappling techniques. Tang soo do means "way of the tang hand," and it uses many spectacular kicks.

Hapkido

Hapkido is a very comprehensive fighting system that teaches punches, strikes, kicks, throws, holds, locks, and pressure point attacks. Hapkido holds, throws, and locks are developed from those used in aiki jujitsu (a form of jujitsu).

This technique is extremely painful, so use it with care.

He immediately releases his hold on you.

Neck hold

You can force your opponent's head into a vulnerable position by attacking him under the jaw.

1 Reach back and dig your thumbs under the angle of your opponent's jaw.

Tang soo do

Students of tang soo do demonstrate the power of their techniques by smashing reusable plastic boards.

Tang soo do kicks

Tang soo do uses a lot of foot techniques, including some impressive jumping kicks.

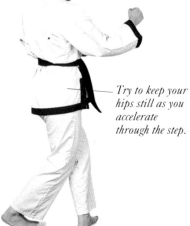

Try to keep your hips still as you accelerate through the step.

The person holding the board must be careful to keep his or her fingers out of the way.

1 Step forward with your left foot, turning your toes outward, and maintaining an effective guard.

Keep your toes pulled back as you kick.

Here the board is being broken by a high roundhouse kick.

2 As you reach maximum speed, move your right knee forward and up, and perform a high front kick.

Attacking a pressure point

You have forced him forward.

2 Keep hold of his head and draw him forward, down, and to the side.

You are attacking the inside of her elbow.

The inside of the elbow is a very sensitive area.

1 Any hold can be made more effective by digging your fingers into a pressure point.

Be careful not to use too much pressure, or you could damage your opponent's elbow.

She has been forced down and onto her haunches.

2 Extend her arm and saw on her straightened elbow with the little-finger edge of your hand.

Three step sparring

Three step sparring is a very safe method for learning about distance, accuracy, and timing.

Deflect the kick with your left forearm.

Attacker aims a kick toward your midsection.

Step away from your attacker with your right foot to avoid the full force of her kick.

1 Your attacker performs a front kick to your midsection. You counter it by quickly stepping back.

Use your right forearm to deflect her kick.

She aims another kick toward your midsection.

Step back with your left foot.

2 She drops the deflected kick forward and performs a second front kick. Step back and force the kick outward.

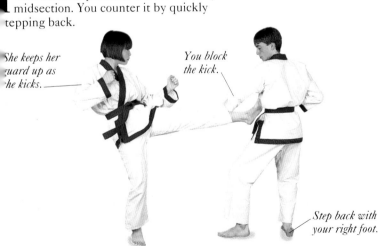

She keeps her guard up as she kicks.

You block the kick.

Step back with your right foot.

3 Then she performs a third and final front kick to your midsection. Step back and block the kick as before.

Her head is unprotected.

Use control and keep your guard up as you perform this technique.

4 Quickly bring your right foot up and around in a roundhouse kick to her head.

Kung Fu 1

K UNG FU is Chinese for "well done," although today the term is used to describe the Chinese martial arts (more correctly called *wu shu*). There are several hundred forms of kung fu. Some are performed in a relaxed way, while others use a lot of power.

The Dragon

He develops his grip so that he can knock incoming techniques out of the way before attacking his opponent.

The Tiger

The Dragon schools of Shaolin kung fu are very powerful styles, using direct attacks and strong techniques against the opponent.

The Tiger uses clubbing and slashing strikes, modeled after those of the wild animal.

Kung fu gates

There are several possibilities for attacking an opponent through areas called the "inside gates" and the "outside gates." A box has been added to this photograph to show these areas.

Outside gates

Inside gates

Inside gates

Attacks on the inside gates come from inside an imaginary box on your body. They are delivered onto your opponent.

Outside gates

Attacks on the outside gates start from outside the box and travel into it.

The Leopard is less aggressive than the Tiger, using the same sort of techniques, but with fewer direct attacks.

The Leopard

She darts in at every opportunity to "peck" at her opponent using her thumb and fingers.

The Crane

The Snake

She avoids her attacker with skillful footwork.

She is about to strike.

The Crane "pecks" at her opponent with strikes made by bringing her thumb and fingers together into a "beak."

The Snake uses her fingertips in a lightning-fast strike, first coiling up and then springing toward her opponent.

Wing chun punches

The wing chun punch uses a throwing rather than a thrusting action. This makes it very effective for people with slight builds. The wing chun punch is famous throughout the martial arts world because it develops a lot of power, even over a distance as short as 1 in (25 mm).

Point your fingers at your target.

Brush your palm with your fingertips.

Clench your fist very tightly. Your thumb should be on top.

Straighten your elbow.

1 For the basic punch, begin by opening your hand and bending your elbow. Now point your fingers at your target.

2 Straighten your elbow and roll your fingers down so that your fingertips brush the top of your palm.

3 Clench your fist very tightly as your elbow reaches full extension. Unlike many other punches, the wing chun punch is made with the thumb uppermost.

You can add power by hunching your shoulders forward behind the punch.

For extra impact, move your body slightly in the direction of the punch.

Use this strike to attack the side of the face, the ribs, or the groin.

You are holding his left wrist so he cannot escape.

You have taken hold of his right wrist with your left hand.

4 The punch travels only a few millimeters, which makes it difficult to block. Impact is made with the lower three knuckles.

Back fist strike

Punches can be made with the backs of the knuckles to attack side-on targets. Use a fast, snapping action.

In the back fist strike, the backs of the knuckles are used and the elbow acts like a hinge.

Kung Fu 2

THE MOST POPULAR forms of kung fu come from the Shaolin Monastery in China. Shaolin monks developed fighting skills to protect themselves from bands of robbers who roamed the country. Later, the monks taught village people how to fight and many new forms of kung fu evolved.

Strikes

Strikes with the hands tend to have less of a sledgehammer impact than punches. Think of them as precision tools applied to "soft" targets, such as the solar plexus or the neck.

Bruce Lee

Bruce Lee is the most famous Chinese martial artist of all time, thanks to his kung fu films. He trained in wing chun kung fu but later developed his own style, which he called *jun fan*. Bruce Lee studied many other martial arts, including Western boxing, and he developed a new system, which he named *jeet kune do* – "the way of the intercepting fist." He died when he was still a young man, but he left behind many films showing his remarkable martial skills.

Opponent's head is forced backward.

Aim the strike up toward his chin.

Opponent's head is forced back by the blow.

Your hand is striking his throat.

This technique must be used with care because it can be dangerous.

Palm heel

The "palm heel" strike is a useful short-range strike that is ideal against the jaw or chin.

Knife hand

The narrow profile of the "knife hand" strike makes it ideal for slipping under your opponent's chin to attack his throat.

Kicks

Wing chun kicks are all aimed at targets below the waist.

Opponent keeps his guard up.

You aim a kick toward his stomach.

Front kick

Raise your kicking knee high off the floor and drive your heel into your opponent's stomach.

You could also drive your heel into his groin or his knee.

Side kick

This time you are sideways-on to your opponent. Lift the foot closest to him and drive your heel down and into his knee.

Keep a firm grip on his wrist as you kick.

Lift your foot and thrust your heel into his left knee joint.

His weight is over his left knee.

Opponent tries to block your strike with his left arm.

You are striking the side of his face with a ridge hand.

Stand with your feet close to your opponent's.

Use the point of your elbow to strike his jaw.

Ridge hand

The "ridge hand" strike uses the thumb side of the knife hand. Use it to attack your opponent's temples, jaw, neck, or groin.

Elbow

The elbow strike is a powerful short-range weapon that clips the point of your elbow across your opponent's jaw, chin, ribs, or breastbone.

Kung Fu 3

CLOSE-RANGE SPARRING demands fast responses. You need to recognize an attack in the blink of an eye, avoid it, and counterattack. You need to make short, economical blocks and fast evasions. The techniques are performed so quickly that you do not have time to think. It takes a lot of practice to develop automatic responses at this sort of speed.

Blocking the person

Kung fu blocks are very sophisticated. Not only do they deflect your opponent's attack and stop it from hitting you, but they also "close off" your opponent so that he or she cannot guard against your counterattack. Chinese people describe this as "blocking the person," not just the technique.

Blocks

The best blocks tend to come from the outside gates, so be prepared to step to the side and turn to face square-on.

The Lion Dance

Kung fu is part of the rich cultural heritage of China. The traditional Lion Dance has close links with kung fu. Each village has its own "lion" that performs a special dance at festival times. The dancers who form the limbs of the "lion" are usually members of the local kung fu club.

Opponent cannot reach with either fist.

You block his punch with the thumb side of your hand.

Stand close to your opponent.

1 You have blocked your attacker's punch. You have knocked his strike across his body, so now he cannot easily use either fist. The block uses the thumb side of your open hand.

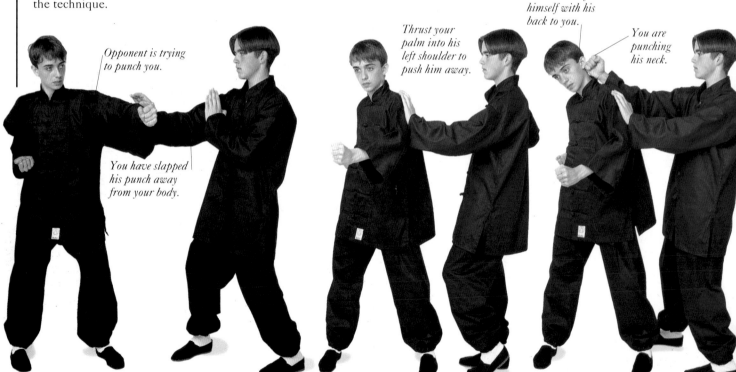

Opponent is trying to punch you.

You have slapped his punch away from your body.

Thrust your palm into his left shoulder to push him away.

He cannot defend himself with his back to you.

You are punching his neck.

1 Use the palm of your hand in a thrusting action to slap your opponent's punch off course and to close him off.

2 Step up with your back foot and thrust your left palm heel hard into his left shoulder, twisting him farther away from you.

3 Now slide your right foot forward and punch your opponent below his left ear. He will find it difficult to defend himself from this turned-away position.

You have blocked his attack.

You are punching him in the ribs.

Try to block the person rather than the technique.

Use the little-finger edge of your hand.

Stand close to him.

His head is turned violently.

You punch him in the side of the jaw.

This punch could produce a knockout, so be careful.

2 As soon as the block makes contact with his forearm, thrust out your left fist and punch him in the ribs. As you become more skilled, there will be less and less time between the block and the punch.

1 Here the block is made with the little-finger edge of your open hand. Your other hand guards from a position where it can quickly grab your opponent's arm if he tries to move away.

2 Close your blocking hand into a fist and punch him in the side of the jaw.

As you block his attack, make sure that you keep your guarding hand up.

Opponent tries to punch you.

He slides in with his left foot.

You step outside his foot.

1 Step to the outside with your leading foot as your opponent slides in and tries to punch you. Take his punch on the little-finger edge of your forearm, just below the elbow, and thrust his punch to one side.

The side of his jaw is the target.

Use your right fist.

2 Grab his wrist with your left (guarding) hand. Now perform a back fist with your right hand, striking him on the side of the jaw.

Kung Fu 4

SPECIALIZED training is essential for close-range fighting. An attack may travel no more than 8 in (20 cm), leaving little time for you to see, recognize, and respond correctly. An advanced form of detection will allow you to counterattack effectively.

Single arm sticking hands

"Sticking hands" is a way of training for close-range fighting. It develops an awareness of your opponent through contact with his arms and hands. The first two sequences are an introduction to sticking hands. Begin slowly and try for good technique rather than power.

Bring your left hand close to your right elbow.

Use your right arm to block his strike.

Bring your right hand up, ready for a back fist.

Use your left hand to grasp his left wrist.

1 Face your opponent and take his left back fist on your right forearm.

2 Grab his wrist with your left hand and draw his arm down and out of the way. Bring your right fist up and prepare to deliver a back fist. Release his left arm.

Double arm sticking hands

This form of sticking hands uses both arms in a rolling action, so you have to sense your opponent's movements through two sets of forearms. Keep up the pressure against your opponent's forearms so that he or she cannot escape or attack you. Move slowly at first and cooperate with your opponent.

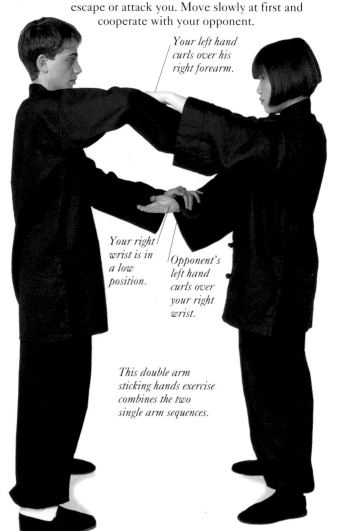

Your left hand curls over his right forearm.

Your right wrist is in a low position.

Opponent's left hand curls over your right wrist.

This double arm sticking hands exercise combines the two single arm sequences.

1 In double arm sticking hands, your arms roll one way and then the other. First your left hand curls over your opponent's right forearm as his hand curls over your right wrist.

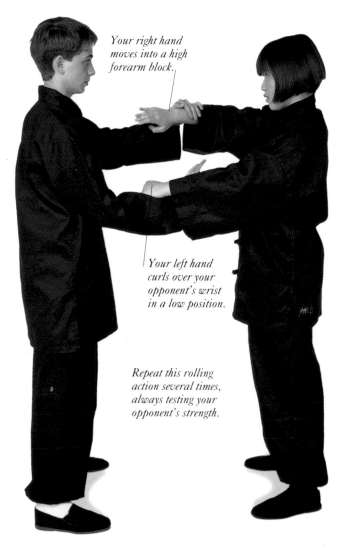

Your right hand moves into a high forearm block.

Your left hand curls over your opponent's wrist in a low position.

Repeat this rolling action several times, always testing your opponent's strength.

2 Then your hands roll so that your right hand moves into a high forearm block while your left hand curls over his wrist in a low position.

He brings his left arm up in a forearm block.

His right hand is guarding his body.

Punch him with your right fist.

Opponent stops your back fist with his forearm.

Curl your fingers over his wrist.

Your fingers point upward.

He tries a low punch.

3 As you attempt your back fist, he brings his left arm up in a forearm block, with his right hand in guard position. Then he grabs your wrist and draws it down, starting the cycle again.

1 Begin the second single arm sticking hands sequence by punching at your opponent with your right fist. He blocks your fist with his left forearm.

2 Then he drops and rotates his left hand into a palm-upward position. You allow your right hand to fall with it, curling your fingers over his wrist.

3 Keep in contact with your opponent's arm. Now he tries to punch you with his left fist and you force it down with your palm heel. From this position you can start the cycle again at step 1.

Draw your left fist back, ready to punch.

Bring your right hand down and grip his right forearm.

Use your left fist to punch him.

He cannot move to avoid your punch.

1 You have spotted a weakness in your opponent's guard. Bring your right hand down to take his right forearm and draw your left fist back, ready to punch.

2 Close him off and punch him in the jaw with your left fist. See how many times you can repeat this sequence without making a mistake.

Wu Shu

WU SHU is Chinese for "martial art." It is a competitive sport in which spears, swords, and unarmed combat routines take the form of dancelike movements. Wu shu teaches flexibility, coordination, self-discipline, and improved concentration.

Set sparring 1

These sparring combinations are taken from set forms in which both opponents have the opportunity to attack and defend. In this sequence, your attacker moves her left foot forward into a low straddle stance as she tries to punch you.

1 Slide your right foot back and block the punch with the little-finger edge of your left hand.

Use the little-finger edge of your hand to force the punch away from your body.

Attacker's feet are wide apart.

You slide your right foot back.

The spear is held with the left hand in front.

Many classical practice forms using the spear still exist today.

Weapons

Training with weapons forms an important part of wu shu. Traditional weapons, such as the spear, were used until the introduction of guns.

Set sparring 3

Gymnastic ability is very important in wu shu competition. Movement is fluid, fast, graceful, and continuous.

Push her fist away from you.

Opponent tries a punch.

1 Step forward on your right foot and thrust your opponent's right fist to the side with your left palm.

The movements of wu shu are very graceful and flowing and there are many spectacular stances.

2 Bring your right foot forward and aim a low kick toward your opponent. She deflects your foot with her right palm. Then she lifts your hand out of the way and prepares for a low kick.

You try a low kick.

Now she aims a low kick.

3 She tries to punch you with her left fist and kick you with her right foot. You move your left foot back as you block both techniques.

Block her punch with your right hand.

Use the palm of your left hand to stop her kick.

Set sparring 2

In this sequence the roles of attacker and defender are constantly switching.

The attacker tries to punch you.

She has stopped your attack by grabbing your right wrist.

You try to strike her across the throat.

She attacks your elbow and tries to over-bend it.

You are forced forward.

1 Your opponent slides her right foot behind her left foot as she tries a sideways punch.

2 Spin around on your right foot and capture her left wrist with your left hand. Then try to strike her across the throat.

3 She sweeps back with her left leg, knocking your right foot back and over-balancing you. She grips your right wrist and presses against your straight elbow.

2 Punch with your right fist, then bring your left knee up and forward, as though you were stepping onto a chair.

Raise your left knee.

Her guard is up, ready to block your punch and your kick.

3 As your left foot touches down, perform a right foot kick as high as you can.

Try to make a splits shape in the air before you bring your right foot down.

The opponent has stepped back to avoid the ax kick.

Freestyle and Thai Boxing

F REESTYLE developed outside Japan and uses karate techniques, but it is much less formal. Freestylists focus on competition and self-defense. Thai boxing, also known as *Muay Thai*, is similar to Western boxing, except that kicks, knee strikes, and elbow strikes are all allowed.

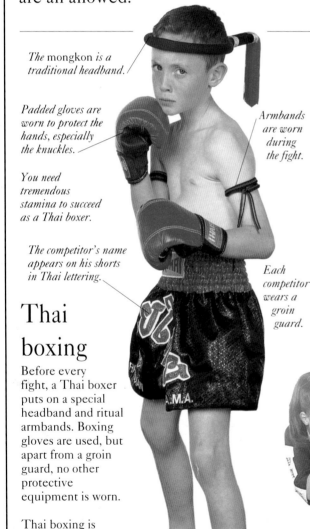

The mongkon *is a traditional headband.*

Padded gloves are worn to protect the hands, especially the knuckles.

You need tremendous stamina to succeed as a Thai boxer.

The competitor's name appears on his shorts in Thai lettering.

Armbands are worn during the fight.

Each competitor wears a groin guard.

Thai boxers compete in bare feet.

Thai boxing

Before every fight, a Thai boxer puts on a special headband and ritual armbands. Boxing gloves are used, but apart from a groin guard, no other protective equipment is worn.

Thai boxing is all about kicking and punching very hard. Punch bags and impact pads are used to develop power, timing, and the ability to judge distances.

Sparring 1

To be good at sparring, you must perform fast, accurate techniques from the correct distance with good timing.

1 You try to punch your opponent's middle. She sees the technique and brings her right hand down to block it.

Opponent has blocked your attack.

You have tried a punch with your right fist.

Your right hip has moved forward behind the punch.

Sparring 2

Only attempt this technique if the floor of the training room will cushion both of you when you land.

1 Face your opponent in a left fighting stance and make sure you have an effective guard.

Opponent

Keep your guard up.

Sparring 3

You cannot expect to win a match with a single technique. Any follow-up must come easily from the first technique, if possible by continuing an existing action. Your opponent lifts her foot, so your leg skims underneath. Then you continue the turn and perform a kick.

She watches you carefully and has guessed your next move.

She has lifted her knee to avoid your attack.

Attempt to sweep her right foot with your left foot.

1 Try to sweep your opponent's leading foot to the side. She sees it coming and lifts her right knee, so your foot skims under hers.

Her attention has been directed downward by your earlier punch.

Her unprotected head is vulnerable to attack.

Use your hip position to perform the roundhouse kick.

2 Perform a high roundhouse kick, curving your foot into the side of her head.

Competitions

Freestyle competition has a lot in common with ITF tae kwon do. Competitors wear fist protectors and strap-on padded boots that prevent damage to the instep.

2 Your attacker attempts a high turning kick to your head. Drop down onto your right hip and jar the back of her supporting leg with your left shin.

Drop down as soon as you see her next move.

Her body-weight is moving up and behind the kick so she is easily unbalanced.

Aim for her calf muscle.

Each foot protector is kept securely in place by two elastic straps.

Big toe strap

Look over your right shoulder.

She keeps her guard up.

Your hips are already in the correct position for a roundhouse kick.

She leans backward to avoid the kick.

2 Continue turning your body and twist to look over your right shoulder. This "winds up" your spine.

3 Allow your hips to follow behind your shoulders and perform a reverse roundhouse kick to her head.

Martial arts around the world

THE PRACTICE OF TRADITIONAL martial arts is no longer confined to the Far East – in fact it is growing in popularity all over the world. Many recent films have sparked an increased interest in the martial arts and knowledge of traditional combat systems is becoming widespread. No single martial art can be regarded as pure: all have borrowed and absorbed each other's techniques and tactics. In time some new fighting arts may even develop, but it is clear that the strong martial arts traditions of Japan, China, and Korea will always continue to thrive.

Shaolin monks

The Shaolin monks are the most famous fighting men in the martial arts world. Over the centuries, many legends have grown up about their heroic exploits. The spectacular shows put on by today's monks are for entertainment and attract huge audiences.

A Shaolin monk displaying his skills

T'ai chi

The Chinese martial art of t'ai chi, which means "great ultimate fist," is now popular all over the world. T'ai chi movements are relaxed and fluid and they are designed to promote health. People who regularly practice t'ai chi hope that the exercises will help them live longer.

Many people in China practice t'ai chi every day

Hwa rang do uses powerful kicks

Thai boxing

Thai boxing is the national sport of Thailand and there are many camps for young boxers throughout the country. Some people believe that Thai boxing is related to earlier, armed forms of combat, but there is no evidence to prove this. Thai boxing is not a martial art in the strictest sense – it is more accurately described as a combat sport.

Thai boxing

Hwa rang do

Hwa rang do is a modern Korean fighting system developed from Japanese and Korean roots. It has a wide syllabus that includes punches, kicks, strikes, locks, holds, throws, and weapons work.

Sumo wrestling

Sumo wrestling is an ancient Japanese form of combat between men of great size and strength that shares some of its origins with jujitsu. An elaborate ritual takes place before every match, often lasting longer than the fight itself. Sumo wrestlers compete inside a 15 ft (4.5 m) circular area and the object is for one wrestler to push the other out of the ring or to make any part of the opponent's body – apart from the soles of his feet – touch the floor. This is achieved by body-charging the opponent, and slapping, pushing, tripping, and throwing.

Sumo wrestlers facing each other before a match

Kobujutsu

Kobujutsu originated on the island of Okinawa, between Japan and China. Police there have traditionally used armed techniques to arrest criminals. Kobujutsu means "old martial techniques," and it describes the practical use of weapons such as the quarterstaff, walking stick, boatman's oar, rice grinder handle, rice flail, and threshing fork.

Kobujutsu

Capoeira is sometimes performed to traditional music

Capoeira

Capoeira is a unique Brazilian form of self-defense developed by African slaves in that country during the 17th century. Rapid kicks are delivered to the opponent's head, the most vulnerable target. Capoeira is sometimes performed to music as a form of entertainment.

Kalaripayit

Kalaripayit is an ancient Indian form of combat that uses both hand-to-hand techniques and weapons such as the walking stick, the staff, and several types of swords and daggers. The unarmed techniques include punches, strikes, and kicks, together with locks, holds, and throws.

Kalaripayit requires tremendous flexibility

Useful addresses

Learning a martial art should be enjoyable, whether you want to compete at a top level or just practice it as a hobby. To get the most out of the experience, make sure you choose a school or club run by a qualified instructor. Below are the addresses of some martial arts organizations and magazines that may be able to help you find a training school in your area.

Young martial arts enthusiasts

General

Aikido Association of North America
5838 Henry Avenue
Philadelphia, PA 19128
ph: 215/483-3000

American Buddhist Shim Gum Do Association
203 Chestnut Hill Avenue
Brighton, MA 02135
ph: 617/787-1506

Kendo students preparing for practice

East/West Martial Arts Academy
255 Tompkins Street
Cortland, NY 13045
ph: 607/756-4961 (or)
1-800-343-9378

International Karate Kobudo Federation
Rt. 61 & Cleveland Avenue
Reading, PA 19605

National Headquarters for United States Matsubayashi-Ryu Karate Do Federation
1718 Queen City Avenue
Cincinnati, OH 45214

Okinawan Seito Ryu International Kei Shin Kan Karate Association
19102 Des Moines Memorial Drive
Seattle, WA 98148
ph: 206/870-0680

Safety America Karate
2595 Cordes Drive
Sugarland, TX 77479
ph: 713/980-3030

Tak Kubota, International Karate Association
3301 N. Verdugo Road
Glendale, CA 91208
ph: 818/541-1240

World Black Belt Bureau Headquarters
708 Germantown Parkway
Memphis, TN 38018

World Shorin-ryu Karate-Do Federation
7425 S. State, Rte. 201
Tipp City, OH 45371

Zen-Do Kai Martial Arts Association, International
P.O. Box 186
Johnstown, NY 12095
ph: 518/762-4723

Magazines

Aikido Today Magazine
Arete Press
P.O. Box 1060
Claremont, CA 91711-1060

Furyu
[The Budo Journal of Classical Japanese Martial Arts and Culture]
Tenegu Press Hawaii
P.O. Box 61637
Honolulu, HI 96839

Journal of Martial Arts
Via Media Publishing Company
821 West 24th Street
Erie, PA 16502
ph: 814/455-9517

Ohara Publications, Inc.
[multiple Martial Arts publications]
P.O. Box 918
Santa Clarita, CA 91380-9018

Organizations/ Training Schools

Aikido Greenwich Village
14-16 Waverly
New York, NY 10003
ph: 212/505-6092

Japan Karate-do Shito-Ryu ITOSU-KAI International
1429 North Bristol
Santa Ana, CA 92760
ph: 714/835-5067
fax: 714/543-5550

New England Small Circle Ju Jitsu Academy
2 Merrill Street
Woburn, MA 01801
ph: 617/932-9366

US Tae kwon do Union
1 Olympic Plaza Suite 405
Colorado Springs, CO 80909

Miscellaneous

YMCA—National
101 North Wacker Drive
Chicago, IL 60606
ph: 1-800-872-9622

Tae kwon do – free sparring

Glossary

When practicing or watching a martial art, you may find it helpful to understand some of the following terms.

A

Application The use of a martial arts technique against an opponent.

Arm lock The application of pressure to the opponent's arm to keep him or her still.

Attention stance A standing position with both feet together and both arms held at your sides. It is used before training begins.

Ax kick A kick with your foot lifted high above the opponent's collarbone, ready to strike with your heel.

B

Back fist A punch using the backs of your knuckles to attack the side of the head or the body.

Back kick A kick behind your body with your back to the opponent.

Ball of the foot The hard part on the sole of your foot just below your toes.

Black belt The term used to describe someone who has passed all the beginner grades of a martial art.

Blocking Stopping the opponent's punch, strike, or kick from reaching your body.

Breakfall A technique for falling safely on your back using one or both arms to soften your landing.

Buddhism An Eastern religion that forms the basis of several martial arts.

Kendo armor

C

Cat stance A standing position with the heel of your leading foot off the floor and your supporting leg bent.

Center of gravity The part of your body around which your weight is evenly balanced.

Chamber position The bent-knee position before your leg is fully extended for a kick.

Closing off Stopping your opponent from attacking by barring his or her arm.

Combination technique The linking of two or more techniques to form a sequence.

Counterattack Any effective defense against an attacking technique.

Cross arm lock An attack used in groundwork to apply pressure to the opponent's elbow until he or she submits.

D

Dan A Japanese word meaning "level."

Do The chest guard worn for kendo.

Dojo A traditional training hall used for the martial arts.

Double lapel grab An attack in which you hold the lapels of your opponent's jacket.

E

Elbow lock An attack in which pressure is applied to the opponent's elbow.

Elbow strike A blow with the point of your elbow.

F

Fighting stance The standing position used for sparring. One foot is slightly in front, both knees are bent, and your fists are raised to guard your body.

Floating hip A throw in which you swing the opponent forward over your hip and onto the mat.

Flying kick Any kick made with both your feet off the ground.

Footsweep An attack used to knock the opponent off-balance by slapping your foot into his or her leg.

Footwork Movements of the feet.

Forearm The part of your arm between your elbow and your wrist that is used for many blocking techniques.

Forward stance A deep, long posture used for performing a lunge punch.

Free sparring A form of training with an opponent that does not use any prearranged movements.

Front kick A basic kick thrusting your foot out smoothly in front of you.

G

Gates of the body The key areas of attack in traditional kung fu.

Gi The traditional jacket worn for many Japanese martial arts.

Grappling techniques Fighting systems that use locks, holds, and throws to defeat the opponent.

Groundwork Techniques such as locks and holds that are performed on a mat.

Guarding Protecting your body against the opponent's attack.

H

Hakama The traditional divided skirt worn for kendo, iaido, and aikido.

Hammer fist A strike with the little-finger edge of the fist.

Karate – a right-hand block

Head block A defense using your forearm to protect your head against an attack.

Head-butt An attack using your head to strike the opponent.

Hogo The special body protector worn for tae kwon do.

Hold A technique used to prevent the opponent from moving and from which it is difficult to escape.

Hooking kick A kick in which your heel curves around to strike the opponent.

I

Inner forearm block A block using the part of the forearm below the little-finger edge of the hand.

Instep The upper part of the foot between the ankle and the toes.

K

Kata A series of movements practiced repeatedly to improve your technique.

Kiai The Japanese word for the shout you make as you strike an opponent.

Kihap The Korean name for the shout you make as you strike an opponent.

Knife block A block using a cutting action with the little-finger edge of the hand.

Knife hand A chopping strike with the fingers held out straight.

Kote The padded gloves worn for kendo.

L

"L" stance A defensive position with most of your weight over your back foot.

Karate – ready for practice

Leg reap An attack that knocks the opponent off-balance by toppling him or her over the supporting leg.
Lock A technique used to hold the opponent still by applying pressure to a joint. Locks can be applied to wrists, elbows, and shoulders.
Lunge punch A punch that uses the weight of your body to add power to your attack.

M

Men The head guard worn for kendo.
Mongkon The traditional headband worn for Thai boxing.
Mune The top section of the body protector worn for kendo.

N

Neck hold A dangerous technique used to hold the opponent still.
Neck throw A throw using leverage against the opponent's neck to swing him or her onto the mat.

Wu shu – a graceful jump

Ninjas Japanese spies highly trained in the art of ninjutsu.
Ninjutsu The ancient Japanese art of camouflage and stealth using secret weapons.
Nunchaku Another name for the rice flail used in kobudo.

O

One step sparring A form of training in which the attacker uses a single agreed technique and the defender uses a prearranged defense.
Outer forearm block A block using the part of your forearm that lies below your thumb.

P

Palm heel A thrusting strike using the base of your palm.
Parry To deflect a punch, kick, or other form of attack.
Prearranged sparring A sequence of movements with an opponent in which you both know all the steps in advance.
Pressure points Sensitive places on the body to which pressure can be applied to force the opponent to surrender.

R

Ready stance A standing position used before you begin sparring. Both feet are apart, knees are straight, and your fists are in front of you.
Rear throat bar Grabbing the opponent from behind and wrapping your forearm across his or her throat.
Reverse punch A punch delivered with the opposite fist of your leading leg.
Reverse roundhouse kick A version of the roundhouse kick in which you hook your heel back into the opponent. It is also known as a reverse turning kick.
Reverse turning kick see Reverse roundhouse kick.
Rice flail A traditional farming tool used as a weapon in kobudo. It is sometimes called a *nunchaku*.
Ridge hand A strike using the thumb side of a knife hand.
Roundhouse kick A curving kick used to strike the side of the opponent's body.

S

Sais Traditional weapons used in kobudo.
Scabbard The hard case used to store a sword and protect its blade.
Scarf hold A hold that traps the opponent's neck with your forearm(s).
Semi-free sparring A form of training in which the attack is decided in advance, but the defense is freely chosen.
Shinai The bamboo practice sword used in kendo.
Shoulder throw Throwing the opponent high over your back.
Side head lock Keeping the opponent still beside you by holding his or her head.
Side kick Thrusting your foot out while your body is turned side-on to the opponent.
Skip front kick Changing your leading leg before you kick.
Snap kick Pulling back quickly when you have finished your kick.
Solar plexus A sensitive area at the pit of your stomach containing many nerve endings.
Sparring A form of fighting with an opponent.
Spent kick (or punch) A kick (or punch) that is finished.
Stance A set position for the body.
Sticking hands A form of kung fu practice for close-range fighting in which your hands and arms remain in constant contact with the opponent's.
Submission When your opponent surrenders to your attack.
Switch change Changing your leading leg in midair as you jump.

T

Taoism An Eastern religion that forms the basis of some Chinese martial arts.
Tapping up When the opponent taps your leg, arm, or the mat to indicate a submission.
Tare The hip protectors worn for kendo.
Tenegui The scarf that is worn under the head guard for kendo.
Three step sparring A form of prearranged practice fighting in which both you and the opponent know the three attacks and defenses in advance.

Kung fu – preparing for a punch

Tonfa A traditional weapon used in kobudo that was originally a farming tool.
Tsuba The handle of the bamboo practice sword used for kendo.
Turning kick A kick that travels horizontally into the target.

V

Vertical back fist A punch using the back of your hand to strike the opponent. The elbow is held low during delivery.

W

Wedging block A block using your forearms against a two-fisted attack by the opponent.
Winding in A technique used in the grappling martial arts to bring the opponent close to your body, ready for a throw.
Wing chun A practical style of kung fu that operates at close range.
Wrist lock An attack in which you apply pressure to the opponent's wrist.

Y

Yin/yang symbol The sign used in Taoism to show the balance of strength with gentleness.

Tae kwon do – a jumping front kick

Index

Acknowledgments
DK would like to thank the following people
for their help in the production of this book:

All the young martial arts enthusiasts and their instructors for giving up their spare time to be photographed for this book.
Sylvio Dokov for allowing us to use photographs from his collection.
Meijin in London for supplying the martial arts uniforms.
Austin Goh of the Oriental Martial Arts Centre in London for lending us the kung fu uniforms and shoes.
James Eldon of the Tang Academy in Plumstead for allowing us to use his training mats.
Paul Clifton at *Combat Martial Arts Magazine* for providing the details of many martial arts organizations.
Sarah Ponder for additional help during the photography sessions.

Thanks to the following young martial arts enthusiasts for modeling:
Aikido
Dale Carter, Richard Gething, and Felicity Poole
Freestyle
Hooda Abu-Gharbieh and Katie Hill
Hapkido
Justin Jules and Felicity Poole
Iaido
Gary West
Jujitsu
Graham Ball, Rebecca Dwayre, Andrew Forrest, and Laura Riley
Judo
Steven Humphreys, Paul Laxton, Gemma Lineham, Ken MacDonald, Jennifer Reeves, Michael Rogers, Joe Tilly, and Sean Thompson
Karate
Christopher Blackledge, Claire Blackledge, Rebecca Cole, Gemma Lineham, and Tom Perry
Kendo
Akihiro Chimoto and Sho Okamoto
Kobudo
Graham Ball, Rebecca Dwayre, Andrew Forrest, and Laura Riley
Kung fu
Dempsey Burvelle, Kassie Landau, Paul Laxton, May Ying Loke, and Michael Rogers
Tae kwon do
Emma Brown, Vaughan Buxton, Martin Eldon, Richard Eldon, and Rebecca Marsh
Tang soo do
Daniel Ayers, Lee Bodell, Paul Laxton, and May Ying Loke

Thai boxing
Rhydian Tolcher-James
Wu shu
Nikunj Chaudhari and Yamuna Chaudhari

Thanks to the following people and clubs for their help:
Aikido
Mr. Jack Poole and Mrs. Marill Poole, Shinwakai UK, Beaconsfield, Bucks
Freestyle
Mrs. Lynne Tolcher-James, The Welsh Academy of Martial Arts, Rhoose, South Glamorgan
Hapkido
Mr. Jacques Jules, UK Sin Moo Hapkido, London
Iaido
Mr. Peter West, Kensei Kai Dojo, Camborne, Cornwall
Jujitsu and kobudo
Mr. Alan Campbell and Mr. Robert Clark, The World Jiu Jitsu and Kobudo Federation, Liverpool
Judo and karate
Mr. Dave Clarke, Mr. Carol David, and Mr. Frank Perry, Busen, Twickenham, Middlesex
Karate
Ms. Paula Mitchell, Phoenix Martial Arts
Mr. Mike Higgins, Lion Karate Association
Kendo
Mr. Jeff Humm, Wakaba Kendo Club, London
Kung fu
Mr. Austin Goh and Mr. Luke Took, Urdang Academy, London
Tae kwon do
Mr. Ron Sergiew, TAGB, Sutton Coldfield
Mr. Ray Gayle, TAGB, Bristol
Mr. James Eldon and Mrs. Sue Eldon, Tang Academy, Plumstead
Tang soo do
Mr. Lewis Loke, British Tang Soo Do Federation, Grays, Essex
Thai boxing
Mr. David Tolcher-James, Rhoose, South Glamorgan
Wu shu
Ms. Krishnaadevi and Mr. Y. W. Lee, United Kingdom Chin Woo Athletic Association, London

Picture credits
key: B bottom; L left; R right; C center T top
Sylvio Dokov: 7TL, 7BC, 18TL, 18 BL, 20TC, 45TR, 58CRB, 59CR, 59CLB, 59BR, 60TR
Ronald Grant Archive: 50TC
Robert Harding Picture Library: 6CL, 6BR, 58BL, 59TL, 60BL
Hutchinson: 7BL
Image Bank: 52CA
Rex Features/Vim Jethwa: 58CA, 58CL
Sporting Pictures: 13TL, 13CLB, 26TC
Tony Stone: 6BL
Werner Forman Archive/Ninja Museum: 7CR; Joe Hloucha Collection: 7TR